# MY LIFE, MY VOCATION

## ONYEMA

# MY LIFE, MY VOCATION

## ONYEMA

# TONY IBENACHO

PRIMIX
PUBLISHING
THE WRITE CHOICE

Primix Publishing
East Brunswick Office Evolution
1 Tower Center Boulevard, Ste 1510
East Brunswick, NJ 08816
www.primixpublishing.com
Phone: 1-800-538-5788

Published by Primix Publishing: 07/28/2025

ISBN: 979-8-89194-509-8(sc)
ISBN: 979-8-89194-510-4(e)

Library of Congress Control Number: 2025912008

# CONTENTS

# INTRODUCTION

This writing is a reflective memoir that chronicles my journey through personal experiences, challenges, and triumphs. Each chapter delves into significant moments that have shaped who I am today. My identity, beliefs, and values are rooted in my upbringing, which continues to reflect and influence my worldview.

Through a blend of storytelling, reflection, and introspection, I explore themes of resilience, love, and the search for purpose. This memoir shares life lessons through poignant anecdotes, offering readers a relatable and inspiring account of overcoming adversity.

As I navigate spiritual formation—from my time with the Marist Brothers and Seminary vocations to career changes and personal growth—I emphasize the importance of embracing vulnerability, determination, and authenticity.

These values were deepened by my academic excellence in Philosophy and Theology, nurtured in the rich intellectual and spiritual environment of the Catholic Seminary.

Ultimately, this biography serves as a testament to the transformative power of self-discovery and the importance of living a life true to oneself.

It encourages readers to reflect on their own journeys, embrace their unique stories, and find strength in their experiences.

**"God often visits us..., but most of
the time we are not at home."**
*(Revelation 3:20)*

# CHAPTER 1

## *Author Biography*

March 2nd 1954, a beautiful nkwo market day, the sun was bright and the birds were singing. My mother was in labor the night before, and my father was at work, but all were anticipating the arrival of a baby. That morning, a bouncing baby boy came into the world and made his family happy. As Theresa and Ben were ardent Christians, hymns of glory to God filled the air at the maternity hospital in Umuokwara Orlu. Friends came up with jubilation songs to welcome the new baby, and as was the norm, any child born on any of the four market days Orie, Afor, Nkwo, eke will be named after the market day, so, my name automatically became Okonkwo after the market day. My parents were ardent Christians whose faith shaped the rhythm of our daily lives.

As was the common tradition, Anna—the second child and only daughter then—was the treasured girl of the family. Our older brother Bon (Boniface) was favored because he was the only son.

My mother had always expressed a desire for a daughter, believing a girl would help her with household chores. When Anna was born, it felt like a prayer had been answered. She quickly became the apple of everyone's eye—until I arrived.

My mother was the heart of our home. She ran a small provision store in front of our house, cared for her three young children, and made daily trips to Mgbede stream—about two miles away—for drinking water. Her days were long and full, but she managed it all with strength and grace.

On market days, she would leave us in the care of our trusted babysitter, Clement Ekemenwee from Umuire village. Clement was a gentle, kind-hearted boy who always tried to please the adults around him. The nearest major market, Eke Eziachi, was about five miles away. My mother owned a beautiful white bicycle, a gift from my father, which she used to cycle to various markets: Eke Eziachi on Eke day, Orie Umuna on Orie day, and Afor Amike on Afor day. Occasionally, my father would give her a ride to more distant markets like Afor Umuaka, Orie Nnempi, Orie Odura, and especially Orie Umuna. She rarely went to Afor Aji, as it often lacked the specific items she needed.

Even during her pregnancy with me, she remained undeterred. She never once fell ill and continued her duties with unwavering energy. Having already birthed two children, she faced this third pregnancy with calm assurance.

The evening I was born, the wind was mild and the sunset gentle—like a quiet spring dusk. When my father received the news at work that his wife had given birth to a healthy baby boy, he rushed to the maternity clinic. Beaming with joy, he exclaimed, "Mrs.—" for that was how he fondly addressed my mother—"I told you it would be a boy!" My mother, smiling, replied, "But this one was different—I never felt the birth pangs like with the others. This boy is indeed special."

News of my birth reached our parish priest and family friend, Father Nwedo, who promptly made arrangements for my baptism. In keeping with tradition, I was first named "Okonkwo," the name given to boys born on a Nkwo market day. Every child received a name based on the market day they were born: Okonkwo (Nkwo), Okorie (Orie), Okafor

(Afor), and Okeke (Eke) for boys; and Mgborie, Mgbafor, Mgbokwo, or Mgbeke for girls.

At my christening, Fr. Nwedo, whose full name was Anthony Nwedo , who later became Bishop of Umuahia Diocese,suggested that I be named Anthony, after his own baptismal name. My mother instantly agreed, noting that her sister's son also bore the same name. My parents both smiled and said, "Yes." And so, I was baptized Anthony.

From the very beginning, I was deeply loved by everyone in the community. Clement, our loyal babysitter, grew especially fond of me and was given the sole responsibility of watching over me as my babysitter. While the other house boys assisted with chores and helped care for my older siblings, Clement was devoted entirely to my care. I was the cherished child, the little one everyone doted on.

# CHAPTER 2

## *My Middle Name:* ONYEMAUCHECHUKWU

The Story of My Middle Name: ONYEMAUCHECHUKWU

The circumstances surrounding my birth were shrouded in mystery and divine intervention. I came into the world —fragile, and clinging to the thinnest thread of life. My mother told me that my birth was miraculous, it was both mysterious and steeped in profound uncertainty. Although the hospital itself in those days was a local facility, ill-equipped compared to the modern standard, and lacking the basic medical tools needed for critical situations, the nurses and midwives were very hardworking and very dedicated, So, the entire community treasured their services and trusted their genuine vocation to help any mother to deliver their children naturally.

As mothers' instincts in a moment of despair are always correct, and looking yet fragile, my mother refused to surrender me to fate. Driven by faith and a fierce maternal instinct, she pulled me close to her chest, whispering urgent prayers to heaven, pleading with God to spare my life.

Then, as if to test the limits of her faith, my tiny body went still. The breath of life, it seemed, had left me, but I was still alive. When my father returned and was told of my uncertain condition, he accepted the word of the Head Midwife. Cradling what he believed to be the uncertainty situation, he acclaimed " fate, or perhaps God, had other plans for this child", that is me.

One quiet Sunday afternoon, Clement—my babysitter—took me along to where his friends were playing soccer. As the game kicked off, he gently placed me in a corner of the compound while he played as the goalkeeper for one of the teams. Left unsupervised, I began to crawl around—curious and unaware of the world's dangers. In my innocent wandering, I ate something I shouldn't have. Not long after, I developed a severe case of diarrhea. When my mother was informed, panic gripped her heart. She immediately urged my father to bring the car out of the garage so they could rush me to the maternity clinic at Umuokwara, about a mile and a half from our home in Umuire village. But on the way to the clinic, I passed out. I stopped responding. I had died. Stricken with grief and believing there was nothing else to be done, my father made a heartbreaking decision—he turned the car around, thinking it would be better to return home instead of going to the hospital with a lifeless child. As they neared the house, something miraculous happened. Just before they got home, my eyes opened—and I sneezed. Startled and overjoyed, my mother exclaimed, "Oh! He is alive!" Without wasting another second, they turned the car around once again and headed back to the hospital. They made it to the clinic successfully, and I was treated. I came back to life. My middle name isn't just a name— it is a name that carries the mystery of my story, a reminder that our lives rest in hands far greater than our own, and that even in the face of death, destiny may yet have other plans.

Remember that somewhere along the dusty path home, a miracle unfolded. My eyes fluttered open. I gasped for air and stirred in his arms. Shock turned to disbelief, then awe. My father rushed back to the maternity ward, clutching me as though I were made of glass. He and my mother begged the staff to do everything in their power to help me live.

Their pleas did not go unheard.

Moved by the sheer will of my parents and the astonishing turn of events, the nurses and staff of the maternity ward rallied around me. They worked tirelessly, sacrificing their time and comfort to nurture me through those critical days and nights. Against all odds, I survived.

In honor of my miraculous return from the brink, my mother gave me the name ONYEMAUCHECHUKWU—a name that carries a profound truth: "Who knows the will of God?"

But that wasn't the only reason I was given the name ONYEMAUCHECHUKWU.

# CHAPTER 3

## *Roots of Discipline and Devotion*

I come from a large family of seven children—five boys and two girls. I'm the third child in the lineup, and the second son. My older sister, Ann and my parents, were especially protective of me during my early years. Growing up in such a close-knit family taught me the true meaning of love and care. The affection and support I received from birth shaped how I treat my siblings today—with the same warmth and devotion that was once showered on me.

In 1960, I started my kindergarten the same year Nigeria became Independent from Britain. The celebration was nationwide and all schools were open for parades in their various stadiums. My parents made my uniform in the pattern of green, white, and green which is the color of the Nigerian flag. Also, the school buildings were painted green, white and Green to mark the celebration. We were ordered to memorize the national anthem. As a kindergarten student, I practiced weekly to be able to recite the anthem when asked unexpectedly by a teacher or the headmaster during the morning assembly. Each morning, the headmaster would have a long list of names of those who would recite the anthem. All was in preparation for the October 1st celebration of the Independence Day of the country. This practice was made part of the daily schedule just to enable students to understand as well as participate in the Independence celebration.

The following year, I was certified to move to the next level known as Elementary One and only those that were accepted into the academy showed great promise. I will never forget my favorite teacher, Mrs. Ekechi from Emekuku Owerri because she was difficult, but was fond of me. This act was demonstrated by the constant questioning and the disciplinary actions inflicted on me. She would always put something in my school box and ask me to give the note to either my mother or my father. Little did I know that was my progress report. Although I was doing very well in her class, I was still playing too much which I later discovered to be her worries. Sometimes she would spank me, and at other times she would sneak notes in my school box and advise me to allow one of my parents to remove it.

Believe it or not, she kept me in line until I graduated from Elementary One, and by then, I had become a well-behaved boy. I'll never forget the lasting impact her firm yet compassionate approach had on my childhood. My grades improved, and my mother was pleased. My father, however—as expected—remained unsatisfied, always pushing me to do more. I never worried much about my school subjects. Still, my father was a strict disciplinarian who never hesitated to flog me, insisting I spent too much time playing. He would often say, "If you spent your time reading and doing your homework after school, you'd be the best in the entire school." In contrast, my physical education teacher used to remind me, "All work and no play makes Jack a dull boy." The tension between those two opposing voices confused me well into my teenage years. Nevertheless, I did my best to strike a balance—studying first, then playing. In my elementary school days, I was both well-behaved and one of the brightest among my peers. My academic success and conduct eventually led my mother to suggest I attend a special school to further strengthen my academic abilities and grow closer to God.

I first became an altar boy in pursuit of the closeness to God that I deeply desired. I believed that part of this commitment meant maintaining purity in all aspects of my life—starting with how I presented myself. I asked my parents for white pants, white shirts, and a pair of white tennis shoes to match, believing that wearing white symbolized the purity I aimed for. Every Sunday morning, I dressed in this outfit to impress not just the ministers and my fellow altar boys, but to embody the reverence I felt for my role. Simply standing at the altar each week made my family proud. More than that, my teachers—who saw me every Sunday—would speak highly of my behavior and academic performance to other students. Their praise boosted my confidence, especially in my academic pursuits.

# CHAPTER 4

## *The Light of Faith In the Shadow of War*

In 1966, the Nigerian Biafra War shattered the peace and stability of the nation, bringing with it fear, chaos, and uncertainty. My childhood dream of becoming a minister was abruptly derailed as the country spiraled into violence. Religious conflict escalated—Muslims slaughtered Christians, and the nation's future grew increasingly bleak. Food became desperately scarce, and survival turned into a daily struggle. Men were drafted into the military, while teenagers, like me, were left vulnerable and without guidance. My older brother was conscripted into the army, and my father did everything he could to protect the rest of us from the dangers closing in.

Each day brought fresh horrors—unrelenting killings, the constant threat of air raids, and the deafening roar of bomber planes and fighter jets overhead. Life in Biafra became unbearable. People died not only from gunfire, but also from rampant disease and starvation, as even necessities like clean drinking water became a luxury. With no safe haven to flee to, communities were overwhelmed by outbreaks of malaria, cholera, and countless unnamed illnesses. The war consumed everything—dreams, lives, and the fragile hope of a better tomorrow.

Although my father was favored in the region because he helped the priests, he never lacked in the relief donations. As a result, he erected a huge garage where food and medicines were stored for anyone that needed such items. Young men and women were hired to distribute the items. So, a lot of people depended on the relief from my father's garage for survival. Yes, we had everything but there was no peace in the land ---- So many families suffered malnutrition nicknamed "Kwashioko".

As a minority in the South, Christians were at a grave disadvantage. The Muslim majority held the upper hand—not only in numbers but also in access to weapons and ammunition—giving them a dominant edge in the war. As the violence intensified, all the white missionaries serving in various parishes fled the country for their own safety. Every day, hundreds of lives were lost in chaos. There was no time or space to properly mourn the dead, let alone bury them. Fear ruled the land, and survival became the only priority. People fled in every direction, each one desperately trying to escape with their life.

Although my parents' spirits were shaken by the chaos of the war, they were never broken. They raised us with unwavering faith—both in our community and in God—and that foundation became the cornerstone of my spiritual growth.

After the war ended in 1970, I began accompanying my parents to daily church services. Near the parish center stood a hospital where my parents took my siblings and me each day to visit those suffering from the war and poverty. The sick and wounded were often brought to the church for healing and physical care. My mother was entrusted with ensuring that none of the injured soldiers went hungry. As a teenager, I assisted her in this mission—helping care for the wounded, praying for their recovery, and offering support in any way I could. We aided amputees, guided those who could barely walk, and provided comfort to the weak and weary.

Essential supplies like clean water and mosquito nets were desperately needed. While the nuns provided the nets, the villagers fetched water daily using buckets. Though my mother led these efforts, I found myself increasingly drawn to the work. Her compassion inspired me, and the desire to help grew stronger within me with each passing day.

Returning to school after the war was a bittersweet experience. While I was joyful to resume my education, I also carried with me the weight of memories from those difficult years. Life was beginning to return to normal, but certain bonds formed during the chaos were hard to forget.

One story from that time still stays with me, etched deeply into my heart. It is the story of Sgt. James—originally known as Musa. He had served on the Muslim side of the military, killing and maiming my people, yet he came to us seeking help and healing after the war. At the parish hospital, where we cared for the wounded and sick, he was tended to by a grieving woman who had lost her only son, James, in the conflict.

This woman showed Musa extraordinary kindness, treating him as though he were her own child. She spoke to him gently, always calling him "James," unable or unwilling to separate her loss from the man in front of her. Touched by her compassion and deeply moved by her pain, Musa eventually embraced the identity she had given him. He chose to be baptized as James, not just in name, but as a symbol of rebirth—a new beginning forged from tragedy and love.

Among the many memories I carry from the post-war period, this act of transformation stands out as a testament to the human capacity for forgiveness and change. Despite the divisions that had torn our nation apart, moments like this reminded me that healing was still possible— through faith, compassion, and the shared pain that makes us human.

"God often visits us…, but most of the time we are not at home" (Revelation 3:20)

# CHAPTER 5

## *Coming to America or A New World, A Harsh Welcome*

Before my departure for America, my father hosted a small gathering in my honor. My mother, teary-eyed, held me tightly and showered me with prayers and blessings. My father, ever composed, advised me to remain a good man and confidently expressed that he believed I would become a worthy ambassador for our family. While I was excited about furthering my education abroad, I was also anxious about leaving behind the familiar comfort of my family and friends to enter a completely foreign land.

When I arrived at JFK Airport in New York, everything felt surreal. The constant electricity alone marked a stark contrast from Nigeria, where power outages were the norm unless a government official happened to be visiting the area. Although I knew no one personally in New York, I had been given a phone number by a friend back home with the instruction, "Call this number as soon as you arrive." I did exactly that, and to my amazement, the voice on the other end was the same friend who had given me the number. He drove all the way from New Jersey to pick me up at the airport.

As I entered his car, the cold struck me like a wall. It was the last week of

17

November, and the temperature had dropped to 42 degrees—unbearably cold for someone who had just left the consistently warm climate of Africa. Noticing my discomfort, he handed me an extra jacket from the passenger seat and said, "I brought this for you. I knew you wouldn't be able to stand this kind of cold. I felt the same way when I first came."

His name was Cletus Obi. He took me to his one-bedroom apartment in New Jersey. His wife was away attending classes, working toward a nursing degree, while their two small children were being watched by a neighbor. That evening, Cletus brought the children home and introduced them to me. Though they were just toddlers, he instructed them to call me "uncle," a role I gladly accepted until their mother returned from school.

Cletus worked as a cab driver, and since his wife didn't yet know how to drive, he would frequently leave work to pick her up from school. They were gracious enough to let me stay with them through the winter, even though my original destination had been Portland, Oregon.

## My Portland Oregon Experience

As my original destination was Portland, Mr. Ken Onyima, who was expecting to see me , came to the airport to give me a ride to his house. Again, the oldest of his children was barely eleven years old.

I was there for about two days and because I was given a room all to myself, his children were literally displaced. So, the second day, his wife did the unexpected. Ken left for work at Gresham and his wife targeted when to carry out her plan to kick me out of the house. First, she asked me to step out of the house. Next, she told me that she forgot her key and asked for my own key as Ken made a key for me. She took my own key and drove off to her business and I was left in the cold-----the hip of snow with no jacket or sweater.

I had nothing on except my sleep wear. I cried my eyes out, and knowing no one except Ken, I walked to a 7—11 store and begged to stay there at least until Ken returned from work. The 7—11 manager, taking pity on me, called a police officer and narrated my situation. The police officer took me to a Haitian man whose son just left to go to school. As soon as I arrived there, his son called and told his parents that he would rather stay another week before actually going back to resume school.

At this juncture, they sent me back to the 7---11 and since the manager had already left for the day, the employee called the corps and the corps called Gresham and narrated what had happened. Ken left his job, rushed down home and took me straight to the airport and I flew back to New Jersey. I thought about choosing the lesser of the two evils.

## *The New Jersey experience continued...*

Prior to my trip to Portland Oregon, Cletus and his wife had discouraged me from going, citing the harsh weather and the lack of support I would find there. What I didn't realize at the time was that the babysitter they had relied on was charging them heavily, and my arrival came as a relief to them.

Gradually, I found myself doing far more than I anticipated. I took care of their children full-time—feeding them, bathing them, washing their clothes—while also contributing financially to the household. For nearly three months, I didn't leave the house except on Sunday mornings for church. I made no phone calls, met no one new, and barely interacted with anyone outside Obi and his immediate circle. His wife was always at school or the library, so I only saw her briefly in the evenings.

Then one day, a guest from out of town visited and spoke candidly with me. He opened my eyes to the reality of my situation: "You didn't come to America to be someone's babysitter. You came here for a purpose, and you're being taken advantage of." His words hit me hard, but they were true.

The following Saturday, I requested a meeting with Obi and his wife before they left for the day. I voiced my concerns and asked them to help me experience more of America beyond their apartment confines. The wife asked me to wait another month until after her final exams. I agreed, but when the time passed with no change, I brought it up again. This time, rather than listen, she became hostile. She threw my belongings out of the house and told me to leave

Cletus Obi Nwachukwu wasn't home at the time and had no idea what had happened until he returned that evening and found me gone.

# CHAPTER 6

## *Homeless in America: The Shelter in New Jersey*

With nowhere else to go and no one to turn to, the homeless shelter became my only option. As I walked through the cold streets, dragging my boxes behind me, I cried quietly—overwhelmed by fear, sorrow, and disbelief. How had I come to this? In a foreign land, full of dreams, I now faced homelessness.

When I arrived at the shelter in New Jersey, I was struck by the sheer number and variety of people crammed into the building. There were individuals of all backgrounds—each carrying their own burdens, trauma, and stories of hardship. Many lived in unimaginable sanitary conditions. The air was thick with unease. Fear, discomfort, and uncertainty filled the space. But I had no choice. If I wanted a place to sleep that night, I had to register.

Later, I needed to use the restroom, and with no means to carry all my belongings, I hesitantly asked two unfamiliar men to watch over my boxes. When I returned just minutes later, both men had vanished—and so had everything I owned. In a panic, I alerted the shelter supervisor. His response shocked me: "I'm not responsible for anything. Go and find out where your stuff is." It was clear I was on my own. I suspected that once they heard my accent, I was perceived as an easy target. I had been robbed—my valuables, clothing, and documents were all gone.

At daybreak, desperate and shaken, I left the shelter and crossed the street to St. Benedict Monastery. I explained my situation to someone there, and I was quickly directed to an African priest. Miraculously, he knew someone from my hometown—though that man lived in Washington, D.C. The priest made a call on my behalf, and the man agreed to take me in. I was put on the next train headed to D.C.

I arrived in Washington at 1:00 a.m. the following morning. My host was a friend of my cousin, a kind-hearted young man named Fred Udemba. A neighboring village in my town Aji. From the moment I arrived, he treated me like family, Igbo cultural values embedded in hospitality. Wherever you see an Igbo person in a foreign land, he/she automatically becomes your brother or sister. He helped me regain my sense of dignity and stability. This time, the weather was kinder, and I was free to step outside, go shopping, and explore the city. For the first time since my arrival in America, I felt like I truly arrived.

Fred quickly discovered that I already knew how to drive, and without hesitation, he encouraged me to pursue my U.S. driver's license. He sent me to the local library to study and prepare for the test. I took the exam, passed it, and walked away with my license in hand—a small but deeply meaningful milestone in my American journey.

"God often visits us…, but most of
the time we are not at home"
(Revelation 3:20)

# CHAPTER 7

## *Through Fire and Fear —*
## *The Road to Resilience*

After being homeless, I moved on with my life and started working — because survival was the only option.

Washing cars at local dealerships was my first real window into American life. Though the work paid just $4.25 an hour, it gave me something more valuable than a paycheck: the chance to interact with people from all walks of life, especially the middle class. It also gave me a sense of direction. Through tireless saving, I managed to buy a fairly used Honda Civic — a real upgrade from the car I used to have. Six months later, I sold it and bought a Nissan Maxima. A man noticed how clean the car was and made me an offer I couldn't refuse. I bought it for $400 and sold it for $800.

Needing transportation to stay afloat, I bought a Mazda 626, fixed it up, and took a job delivering pizzas for Pizza Hut on Rhode Island Avenue. That job, however, nearly cost me my life.

One night, I received a delivery order to a non-existent address. As I circled the neighborhood searching for the house number, a young man approached. Before I could even ask for directions, he pointed a gun at my temple. He demanded all the money in my pocket. I complied without resistance. Trying to keep him distracted, I told him there were more pizzas in my car if he was hungry. As he turned toward the vehicle, I took off running like my life depended on it — because it did. He fired two shots at me. I wasn't hit, but I fell hard, bruising my knee and ankle, blood running down my legs.

Shaken and terrified, I hobbled back to the Pizza Hut. My manager, a fellow Nigerian, barely looked at me before demanding the delivery money. That was the last straw. I quit on the spot. There was no insurance, no support — only risk. I filed a police report and later learned that the young man had been caught driving my stolen car the next day. Still, I refused to testify. He was part of a gang, and cooperating with police would've made me a marked man.

The trauma lingered. I remained indoors for weeks, paranoid and afraid to step outside. Eventually, I took a job at another car dealership, this one also on Rhode Island Avenue in D.C. To stay close to work, I rented a basement room behind Mills Avenue. The landlady was cruel and cheap. She heated only the top floor with firewood and charged me $350 a month, constantly reminding me that I was getting a $50 discount — only because I chopped her firewood after work. I nearly caught pneumonia in that cold, damp basement.

Two months of enduring her meanness and freezing nights were enough. I moved to a small room in Adelphi, Maryland, and started a new job at Wendy's. But even as I settled into a new routine, my heart remained back home. I ached to see my family. Loved ones began passing away — one after the other. I recorded messages on cassette tapes to send home, and my family did the same. Hearing their voices, their tone, their laughter and sorrow gave me strength — and broke my heart.

Then came the news that shattered me: my father had died. What made it even more painful was that he had sent a tape, asking me to buy him specific items. I bought every one of them, placed them in the trunk of my car, and waited for Fr. Onyima's return to Nigeria so he could take them home. That day never came. Those items stayed in my trunk for three years until I eventually gave them away to the Salvation Army.

I had never properly grieved my mother, who passed away a year before my father. She couldn't live without him. Losing them both while I was so far away made it impossible to find closure.

After quitting Wendy's, I took a job as a security officer at the Chateau Apartments in Silver Spring, Maryland. I also went back to washing cars. At one point, I juggled three jobs just to recover lost time — and money. I was saving about $3,000 every three months.

With growing confidence, I applied to teach at a Catholic school. They hired me and sent me to Southeast D.C. to teach 7th grade. Nothing could have prepared me for that classroom. The students' behavior was wild and exhausting. It was my first time standing in front of American teenagers, and their chaos nearly gave me a heart attack.

Still, something inside me had shifted. I was no longer just surviving. I was beginning to imagine a future — maybe even owning a home. But I had no idea how to start.

# CHAPTER 8

## *Never Be Homeless Again*

Going through different struggles and juggling various jobs was incredibly difficult. Some of the work was risky, physically demanding, and emotionally draining. The challenges I faced only deepened when I learned that both of my parents had passed away. That moment shattered me. It was one of the darkest periods of my life. Overcoming those obstacles wasn't easy—but I knew I had to keep pushing forward. I had to survive.

Eventually, things began to shift. I bought my first home and made a vow to myself that I would never be in that situation again.

In 1997, the house at 6307 Kennedy St., Riverdale, Maryland was listed for sale. The listing agent, Mike Oputa, a native of Ogbaru, encouraged me to gather my pay stubs and connected me with a lender. With his help, I was able to secure a loan and purchase the property—a modest three-bedroom, one-bath house—for $97,000.00.

At the settlement table, tears streamed down my face as I signed the paperwork. No one around me truly understood why I was crying—but I did. After a long and painful journey through homelessness, rejection, and hardship, I was finally holding the keys to a place I could call my own in America. On every document I signed, I wrote the words: "Never Be Homeless Again."

At first, I lived in the unfinished basement while renting out the upstairs bedrooms to tenants—John, his younger brother, and another man. Within two months, I completed the basement and installed a full bath. Determined to stay within legal bounds, I obtained a license to lease the property from PG County.

That house became the start of a new chapter. I began buying, renovating, and selling homes throughout Maryland. Over the years, I housed many tenants and continued to build not just a livelihood, but a future rooted in stability and dignity.

After achieving one of the greatest milestones of my life—owning a home in America—it felt like the right time to return to where it all began. It was time to go back home to Africa.

This was my first trip back since leaving, and the excitement was overwhelming. I was to visit home for the very first time, friends mailed boxes and boxes full of items and of course sent the excess baggage payment. I documented the journey, including my heartfelt intention to visit my parents' graves—a moment I had waited for, through years of struggle and longing.

When I arrived, it was as if the entire village came alive. Many thought I was either lost to the world or would never return. My arrival brought an outpouring of emotion—cheers, hugs, tears of joy. Music filled the air, and spontaneous dances broke out in celebration. The happiness was contagious.

There was no denying it—I was home. And this time, I returned not just as the person who left, but as someone transformed by perseverance, purpose, and hope.

That homecoming rekindled something within me—a reminder of

where I came from and who I was meant to become. With that clarity, I returned to the U.S. more committed than ever to live a life of purpose.

As I move forward from past experiences, I find myself returning to the core of my original purpose. At that time, I was inexperienced and unaware of many complexities, but one thing was always clear—my deep desire to serve the sick and support those in need. This calling led me to train and become certified as a Certified Nursing Assistant (CNA).

Since 1998, I have been teaching in Special Education, a field that aligns with my passion for care and service. Currently, I teach a class of 13 students, ranging in age from 14 to 18, each with unique challenges. My students live with conditions such as Autism, Intellectual Disabilities, ADHD, physical impairments, and Bipolar Disorder, etc.

While there are many areas of specialization within education, I chose this path deliberately. Becoming certified in this field has empowered me to continue my mission—working with the sick, supporting the underserved, teaching, and providing guidance. Through this work, I am honored to engage with and learn from individuals across all walks of life.

# CHAPTER 9

## *Where Ministry Meets Humanity*

After acquiring a home and overcoming many personal struggles, I can now say that the dreams I once held are gradually becoming a reality. One of those dreams—rooted in a deep desire to care for the sick—led me to become a Certified Nursing Assistant.

Even before my desire to serve people in healthcare, I felt a strong calling to ministry.

Following my secondary education, I pursued theological studies and earned a degree in Divinity from Bigard Memorial Seminary. I further deepened my knowledge by completing a Master's degree in Theology at the Catholic Institute of West Africa, with a specialization in Pastoral Theology. These academic and spiritual experiences reinforced my belief that I have a vocation to help those in need. That same calling is clearly reflected in my current work in Special Education.

Driven by a profound passion for service, I enrolled in Clinical Pastoral Education (CPE)—a unique training designed for those who feel called to grow in pastoral competence. I view CPE as a transformative journey that prepares one to serve humanity from the heart. It brings out the best in individuals with a genuine vocation for compassionate service.

Throughout my CPE program, I dedicated myself to enhancing my pastoral effectiveness. I firmly believe that acquiring pastoral skills requires hands-on experience in a clinical setting under skilled supervision. My goal is to become a competent spiritual caregiver— someone who can self-reflect and provide meaningful spiritual support to patients, their families, and hospital staff.

Before undergoing CPE, I often approached pastoral ministry from the head. Now, I serve from the heart. This training has not only shaped my approach to ministry but has also helped me discover a deeper understanding of myself. Through Pastoral Education, I have come to truly know Anthony.

# CHAPTER 10

## *Years Wasted and Lost*

After all the dreams and aspirations, I finally found myself — the real me. But life, as always, has a way of humbling even the most determined. I lost my way again.

Coming out from the church, I was innocent, unexposed to the realities of the world. Naïve. I didn't know much about women or the ways of the world outside spiritual life. Then, someone from my local government area suggested I marry his cousin, a woman living in Dallas, Texas, while I was based in Maryland at the time.

She came to meet me, determined that we must marry — captivated not by love, but by the life I had built. I was doing well: seven registered cars, a stable career, and plans to continue in religious service. But she saw something else — my vulnerability.

I trusted her. I let her in. I thought I was building a life, but I was being led into a trap.

Before our marriage could happen, she traveled to Nigeria, supposedly to meet my family and formalize our union. Although the traditional rites (Igba Nkwu) were performed, her clandestine agenda was undisclosed.

While there, she reconnected with her boyfriend, a medical doctor, and became pregnant by him. When she returned, she told me the child was mine. I believed her. I celebrated. I wrote. I published. I planned our future around this child.

Then everything unraveled.

When she went to Nigeria, again, she took everything — not just physical possessions, but years of my work. A brand-new Mercedes I shipped there. Building materials. Land I had purchased. She made an effort to change the land documents from my name to her older brother's name — a calculated move. I later learned she planned to kill me so they could take over everything.

Back in the U.S., while I was out teaching one day, she emptied our home. She left only the food on the stove and a few documents. She made away with — my certificates, my transcripts, my video documentary, and because we had a joint account, she cleaned everything in the account and left me with nothing. She had rented a new apartment with another man. I was broken.

I searched for her and the baby. I pleaded. She refused to return. Instead, she took me to court, claiming all sorts of false accusations. But God, as always, stepped in. The judge saw through her lies and ordered a DNA test. The result shattered me: the child was not mine.

That discovery pushed me to the brink. Depression hit hard. Meanwhile, she was telling her friends I was suicidal. She pretended to return, pretending to reconcile. She brought food, poisoned food — heavily laced and intended to kill. That night, she kept calling, checking if I had eaten.

But I hadn't. As a man of prayer, I prayed over the food before eating. Something didn't feel right. I placed the food on the balcony. Soon, two black birds appeared. They devoured the food quickly. One dropped dead instantly; the other flew away, but I knew it wouldn't make it far.

That was my sign. That could have been me.

I collapsed on my knees and wept. I thanked God for saving my life again.

She came back once more, begging for forgiveness, pleading to return. But friends warned me: She's coming to finish what she started.

This confirmed that the human serpent came to exploit, extort and to kill. I vested all my human and spiritual resources into what I thought was love and family. After five painful years, the truth revealed itself. I lost everything — investments, personal belongings, and the life I worked so hard to build.

But from the lion's den, I rose.

Desperate and unaware, I had become prey to someone who saw my vulnerability as an opportunity. I moved everything to Texas — my house, my savings, my life — all under the illusion of love. From Arlington to Lewisville, the manipulation intensified until it climaxed with attempted murder.

She poisoned my food and spread false stories of depression and an impending suicide. But God intervened.

Two black birds ate the food. One died, and the other fled — a living metaphor of what I had escaped.

Yes, I lost years. I lost my possessions. I lost trust. But I did not lose hope.

God preserved my life for a reason.

# CHAPTER 11

## *A Challenging Year,*
## *2019–2020*

The challenge didn't stop there. After I was lost, more misfortunes followed.

Parkland Hospital used me for an experiment, but my God said no. I was almost paralyzed as they experimented on my pain. The torn muscles were the result of a fall on the tennis court. I belong to the Nigerian Tennis Club in Dallas and have served as the Honorable Secretary for three terms — first under the Anuwe administration, next under Ike Iwunna, and finally under Cosmo Okoro.

While at Parkland, pain injections were constantly administered to manage the pain from my torn muscle, but the pain never subsided. I even advised them to amputate my left limb, but one of the nurses objected to the idea.

Eventually, I was transferred to the neighboring hospital — UT Southwestern — where I was admitted by an Indian doctor who advised that I be taken home. The reason? Pain medication had been over-administered in my system, and any additional dose could have killed me instantly. Her actions gave me probable cause to trust her professional advice. Her name was Dr. Nandivada, a very pretty lady who appeared considerate and sincere. She said, "Take him home. They were trying to kill this man with pain medicine." She promised to help with the healing process and to continue sending medication to support my recovery.

While at home, I couldn't sit in a chair or lie down on any bed. Sleeping lasted only five minutes at a time, and the pain was constant. Climbing stairs was impossible. Walking was nearly unbearable. The Nigerian Catholic Men Organization (CMO) saw my condition and paid me a recovery visit.

This condition lasted for almost a year. As a result, I was forced to retire and leave teaching.

# CHAPTER 12

## *Back to my Teaching Job and the Presence of my Children*

After facing near-paralysis—unable to sit or even lie down properly—I eventually got back on my feet. I was being pressured to retire and leave the teaching profession, but my God did not allow me to remain stuck in that moment. Instead, I was blessed with a new chapter: the gift of a loving wife, and later, the joy of becoming a father to a beautiful daughter.

Fearing that I was 'passing away' without someone to call my own—and after spending three quarters of my life caring for other children—I made a move to adopt children from Nigeria. With my wife's cooperation, we went home and adopted two children: Uzoma Tony Junior and Urenna Ada Ibenacho. And because children invite other children, my wife conceived and we had a beautiful girl: Juliant Zikora Ibenacho. The names signify the combination of Juliana and Anthony. Zikora means "Show the world that you are God." In other words, God has shown the world that He is a wonderful God indeed. Zikora was born in August 2021, the same year I finished my online Doctoral degree program. The Nigerian Tennis Club and the Umuakah community in Dallas, TX were invited to celebrate these abundant blessings.

Staying home to care for Zikora and build that precious father-daughter bond filled my heart completely. During this time, my wife Juliana returned to work as an RN service provider at White Rock Medical Facility. When Zikora grew strong enough to attend daycare, we explored several facilities—but none met our expectations. Some even mistreated our precious angel. Discouraged and frustrated, we spent months searching, until we found a daycare just five minutes from our home in Mesquite. There, Ms. Bunny listened to our concerns and treated our daughter with genuine love and respect. Later, Ms. Brandy continued the same high standard of care that Zikora deserved.

While all this was unfolding, Dallas ISD reached out and offered me a DOI (District of Innovation) position in Special Education. I was assigned to Joe May Elementary School, where I was warmly welcomed and appreciated. After a successful first year, I was transferred to Gabe P. Allen Elementary, where I continued to thrive professionally. Later, I was required to complete a high-level course known as the Reading Academy—and I succeeded, earning my certification and further advancing my teaching career.

# CHAPTER 13

## *The Simultaneous Death of My Siblings*

But life is not all about happiness, opportunities, and success. Life is truly a balance—a mixture that includes sadness and discouragement.

My immediate older brother, Eze Sir Boniface Ibenacho, the Traditional Ruler of Aji Autonomous Community, died, and my immediate younger brother, Joseph, passed away just three weeks apart. They were both buried on December 19th and 20th, 2024. I was devastated and fell into depression because, out of seven children, three are now gone—just like that. First was my immediate older sister, Anna, and now Bon and Joseph. Left to mourn them are myself, Emmanuel, Emeka (Paschal) in Hong Kong, and Sr. Maria.

To help with the funeral arrangements of my brothers, the men in the Ibenacho compound formed a WhatsApp group forum, and I became the president of the forum.

Now, although I still go to work, serve my Dallas community and engage in church activities and help my family, my strength is dwindling day by day. I constantly donate funds to my hometown parish in Aji for the construction and installation of pews and tiles on the entire church floor, in commemoration of my late parents, Benedict and Theresa Ibenacho. I consider myself blessed as I still believe that whatever happens in life, not only that God knows about it, yet He allows it to happen. His will is what counts and not our human assessment. I am therefore grateful for His grace and protection. May He be praised both now and forever.

"God often visits us..., but most of the time we are not at home" (Revelation 3:20)

www.ingramcontent.com/pod-product-compliance
Lightning Source LLC
Chambersburg PA
CBHW031238120626
46545CB00003B/1174